The Haymarket Affair: The History of the Riots in Chicago that Galvanized the Labor Movement

By Charles River Editors

A contemporary engraving of the Haymarket Affair

About Charles River Editors

Charles River Editors provides superior editing and original writing services across the digital publishing industry, with the expertise to create digital content for publishers across a vast range of subject matter. In addition to providing original digital content for third party publishers, we also republish civilization's greatest literary works, bringing them to new generations of readers via ebooks.

Sign up here to receive updates about free books as we publish them, and visit Our Kindle Author Page to browse today's free promotions and our most recently published Kindle titles.

Introduction

A sympathetic engraving commemorating the "anarchists of Chicago" and the defendants in the trials after the Haymarket Affair

The Haymarket Affair

"That night I could not sleep. Again I lived through the events of 1887. Twenty-one months had passed since the Black Friday of November 11, when the Chicago men had suffered their martyrdom, yet every detail stood out clear before my vision and affected me as if it had happened but yesterday. My sister Helena and I had become interested in the fate of the men during the period of their trial. The reports in the Rochester newspapers irritated, confused, and upset us by their evident prejudice. The violence of the press, the bitter denunciation of the accused, the attacks on all foreigners, turned our sympathies to the Haymarket victims." – Emma Goldman

Although it's no longer well known as a flashpoint, few things were as controversial during the late 19th century as the Haymarket Affair. Depending on one's perspective, the riots and the violence that ensued were the result of anarchist terrorists attacking law enforcement authorities with a homemade bomb that was detonated during a large public event, killing a police officer and wounding several more. Others who were more sympathetic to the plight of the people protesting for better working conditions that night in Haymarket Square in Chicago on May 4, 1886 portray it as a peaceful rally that was marred by a heavy handed response attempting to disperse the protesters.

What is clear is that the moments following the explosion were characterized by confusion and bedlam, as some people ran away and others ran toward the site. By the time the shooting was done, nearly a dozen lay dead, including a number of police officers, and makeshift hospitals were soon overwhelmed.

Citizens in the area began to cry out for justice, and police detectives poured through the city, making arrests and questioning thousands. As word spread about the attack, cities around the country went on high alert, concerned that they could be next. It was soon determined that a traditionally anti-American group was responsible for the attack, and many threatened mob violence against anyone who looked like they might be involved with the group. The press egged on those in the public with cries for revenge and justice. Eventually, the suspected perpetrators' trial began, a sensational event followed closely by many across the nation. Tensions ran high as those involved were prosecuted and defended, and when the jury convicted 8 anarchists of conspiracy and some of them were sentenced to death, many rejoiced while others cried out that Lady Justice had miscarried the case.

Lost amidst the violence was the fact that the protests that culminated with the Haymarket Affair had come in response to previous labor strikes across the country, and controversial police shootings of some workers on strike, which took on a discriminatory undertone because many of the laborers were immigrants facing poor working conditions. It was against this backdrop that political anarchists also got involved, which muddled things and ultimately brought blowback against immigrant communities after the Haymarket Affair.

More importantly, workers and those advocating on their behalf were galvanized by the events to push for what they considered much needed reforms, many of which would come over the next few decades. As professor William J. Adelman put it, "No single event has influenced the history of labor in Illinois, the United States, and even the world, more than the Chicago Haymarket Affair. It began with a rally on May 4, 1886, but the consequences are still being felt today." Chicago has since commemorated both the workers and the police with various memorials and plaques.

The Haymarket Affair: The History of the Riots in Chicago that Galvanized the Labor Movement chronicles the turbulent events that led to the controversial protests, and the impact they had after the dust had cleared. Along with pictures of important people, places, and events, you will learn about the Haymarket Affair like never before, in no time at all.

The Haymarket Affair: The History of the Riots in Chicago that Galvanized the Labor Movement
About Charles River Editors
Introduction
    Chapter 1: If the Workmen Are Organized
    Chapter 2: Premonitions of Danger
    Chapter 3: Indicted for the Murder
    Chapter 4: Come Into Court
    Chapter 5: They Are Putting On the Caps
Online Resources
Bibliography

Chapter 1: If the Workmen Are Organized

"Six months ago when the eight hour movement began, there were speakers and journals of the I. A. A. who proclaimed and wrote: 'Workmen, if you want to see the eight hour system introduced, arm yourself. (If you do not do this, you will be sent home with bloody heads and the birds will sing May songs upon your graves.' 'That is nonsense,' was the reply. 'If the workmen are organized they will gain the eight hours in their Sunday clothes.' Well, what do you say now? Were we right or wrong? Would the occurrence of yesterday have been possible if our advice had been followed?

Wage workers, yesterday, the police of this city murdered at the McCormick factory so far as it can now be ascertained, four of your brothers, and wounded, more or less seriously, some 25 more. If brothers who defended themselves with stones (a few of them had little snappers in the shape of revolvers) had been provided with good weapons and one single dynamite bomb, not one of the murderers would have escaped his well merited fate. As it was, only four of them were disfigured. That is too bad. The massacre of yesterday took place in order to fill the forty thousand workman of this city with fear and terror---took place in order to force back into the yoke of slavery the laborers who had become dissatisfied and mutinous. Will they succeed in this? Will they not find at last that they miscalculated? The near future will answer this question. We will not anticipate the course of events with surmises." - "Blood," an article published in the *Arbeiter-Zeitung*, May 4, 1886.

While it may be true that every cloud has a silver lining, it is equally true that progress rarely comes without a price. During the decade that followed the end of the Civil War in America, the North experienced a period of unprecedented industrial growth, and most of the men taking jobs in these new factories came from one of two backgrounds: either they were former soldiers hardened by four years spent at war, or they were European immigrants, hardened by a lifetime of suffering. Either way, they were a determined group who soon tired of working from dawn 'til dusk for little money and less respect, and by 1867, many in Chicago and other large cities had organized themselves into unions and were beginning to fight for a better life, not only for themselves but for their families.

As a result, on March 2 of that year, the governor of Illinois signed the first law in American history to limit adults to working only 8 hours a day, but unfortunately, many employers did not care for the new law and refused to obey it. Local politicians would not send officers out to enforce something they themselves did not believe was right. The infant labor movement failed to grow, and the Gilded Age of the haves and the have nots got off to a solid start. Then, just a few years later, the face of Chicago changed when a substantial part of the city burned down during the Great Chicago Fire of 1871.

Millions of Americans and immigrants had moved west during the mid-19th century to grab land, especially after President Lincoln signed the Homestead Act in 1861, and the ability to get to Chicago by rail or sea made it a popular destination. Similarly, in the wake of the fire, European immigrants poured into the rebuilding city and soon rose to places of political prominence. Albert Parsons and his wife, Lucy, also moved to Chicago during this period, but from Texas, and Parsons began encouraging the men around him to join his new Social Democratic Workingmen's Party. Over the decade that followed, tensions between the party and the police slowly grew from mild aggravation to occasional violence.

Albert Parsons

Lucy Parsons

Although Illinois had been progressive in implementing the 8 hour work day, workers had been lobbying the federal government on the issue, and the Federation of Organized Trades and Labor Unions agreed that workers should demand 8 hour work days as a standard in unison beginning on May 1, 1886. With that, hundreds of thousands of workers began their strikes as that day approached, chanting slogans such as "Eight-hour day with no cut in pay." Chicago was no different, with estimates of 10,000 workers in the city striking in protest and marching at the beginning of May. With that, the stage was set for a major incident.

The events that brought about the Haymarket Affair began in earnest on May 3, when August Spies, a disciple of Parsons and editor of the German-language newspaper *Arbeiter-Zeitung* ("Workers' Times"), led a rally of several thousand striking workers near the McCormick Harvesting Machine Company plant. Many of the employees there were Irish immigrants, and they had already been mistreated by law enforcement during past strikes, which only heightened tensions there. In fact, replacement workers at the plant already had hundreds of police on site to ensure they could cross the picket lines and make it to their jobs.

Among the speakers that day was Fritz Schmidt, a Socialist from the Central Labor Union. He incited the marchers, shouting, "On to McCormick's and let us run every one of the damned scabs out of the city. It is they who are taking the bread from you, your wives, and your children. On to then blow up the factory, strike for your liberty. This could be done with the revolver, the bludgeon dynamite, and the torch…strike for your freedom and if the armed murderers of the law interfere shoot them down as you would the 'scabs.' Revolution is the only remedy. Do not be afraid - arm yourselves. Use the torch and protect your rights. Be men. Arm yourselves and get what rightfully belongs to you."

Spies

When the replacement workers, who Schmidt and the striking workers denigrated as scabs, tried to leave for the day, a confrontation broke out and soon grew out of control. According to a May 4 article in the *Chicago Tribune*, "'On to McCormick's,' cried the mob, and a number began moving in that direction, but were called back by several of the cool-headed strikers, who took Fritz down from the car and held him to get out of the vicinity. Just then the factory bell rang, and the mob, moved by a common impulse, started on a run toward the big gates which face Oakley Avenue. It was a race of only two locks and the head of the mob reached the gates just as the men began to come out. In the run such of the mob as was not already provided armed itself with stones. When the men walked out of the gates the stones began to fly. The men dodged the missiles as best they could, and ran while their fellow workmen, who were still in the yard, retreated to the shops. The stones flew thick and fast; and above the mad roar of the mob rose the crash of breaking glass as the windows went in. Fifty men and boys swept in through the gates and in a flash looted the gatekeeper's house of everything there was in it. The company has kept a dozen guards at the works ever since the strike, a few weeks ago and these, when the mob reached the gates, fired their revolvers in the air, hoping to frighten the attacking party off. The strikers laughed at this and amused themselves by pelting the guards with stones till they too retired. Then they followed them up and began battering sown the doors with crowbars. At this moment a patrol wagon loaded with officers was seen approaching."

Naturally, it did not take long for the police to respond. According to the *Tribune*, "Showered with stones and bricks, the officers crouched low in the wagon which turned sharply off the avenue and ran down toward the gate. As the wagon drew up before the gate the policemen jumped off and drawing their revolvers and leveling them at the approaching men, held them at bay. … The crowd again advanced a short distance and pelted stones and other missiles. … It seemed as if the majority of them were armed and revolvers of every sort flashed in the sun. A volley was poured into the little band of 12 policemen the patrol in the meantime standing inside the yards of the factory. Occasionally when the rioters got dangerously close, a volley was fired by the police, but the officers generally shot to scare and not to kill. … One stray shot struck the boy Joseph Votjek in the groin. Shots were flying back and forth, but the strikers were bad marksmen…More police were summoned and until they arrived the 12 held the mob at bay. It is known that at least a dozen men were wounded and some quite seriously, but their friends carried them off. When reinforcements reached the ground the police formed and by a determined effort, scattered the mob. Once broken, the men fled in every direction. A dozen were captured and taken to the police station and locked up on the charge of riot. Many of McCormick's workmen were assaulted and slightly injured. Patrolman Casey was sent to Vojtek's house to tell his family he was injured. There he was surrounded by a mob and a rope brought out to hang him. A detail of police came to his rescue…"

A couple of workers were killed, and Spies complained that the police response had been an attempt to intimidate the protesters and break their resistance: "I was very indignant. I knew from experience of the past that this butchering of people was done for the express purpose of defeating the eight-hour movement." But in spite of the violence, or perhaps because of it, both sides' stances only hardened, and the *Tribune* noted that the factories remained determined to stand their ground on the issue of the length of the workday: "The managers of all the roads running into this city today met and discussed the eight hour movement as far as the railroads are at present affected by it. It was unanimously resolved that all the roads centering in the city should act in concert; that no reduction in hours or an increase in wages be granted at this time the business and condition of the roads being such that neither concession could be made: that all refusing to go to work tomorrow morning will be promptly discharged and new men put in their places, and that the authorities be requested to give the roads such protection as will enable them to carry on their business."

Chapter 2: Premonitions of Danger

"Sam Fielden began by saying that there were premonitions of danger. All knew it. The press said the Anarchists would sneak away. They were not going to. [Applause.] If they continued to be robbed it wouldn't be long before they would be murdered. There was no security for the working classes under the present social system. A few individuals controlled the means of living, and they held the workingman in a vise. Everybody doesn't know that. Those who knew it were tired of it, and knew the others would get tired of it too. They were determined to end it, and would end it, and there was no power in the land that could prevent
them. [Applause.] Congressman Foran had said the laborer could get nothing from legislation. [Applause.] He also said that the laborers could get some relief from their present condition when the rich man knew it was unsafe for him to live in a community where there were dissatisfied workmen; that that would solve the labor problem. [Applause.] The speaker didn't know whether they were Democrats or Republicans, but whichever they were they worshiped at the shrine of rebels. John Brown, Jefferson, Washington, Patrick Henry, Hopkins said to the people, the law is your enemy; we are rebels against it. The law is only framed for those that are your enslavers. ['That's true.']" - *Chicago Tribune*, May 5, 1886

In the immediate aftermath of the fighting near the plant on May 3, anarchists in the area began to circulate a flyer calling for protesters to head to Haymarket Square the next day. Ominously, they called upon the marchers to arm themselves, which would increase the potential for a similar, violent confrontation.

Attention Workingmen!

GREAT
MASS-MEETING

TO-NIGHT, at 7.30 o'clock,
AT THE
HAYMARKET, Randolph St., Bet. Desplaines and Halsted.

Good Speakers will be present to denounce the latest atrocious act of the police, the shooting of our fellow-workmen yesterday afternoon.

Workingmen Arm Yourselves and Appear in Full Force!

THE EXECUTIVE COMMITTEE.

Achtung, Arbeiter!

Große
Massen-Versammlung

Heute Abend, ½8 Uhr, auf dem
Heumarkt, Randolph-Straße, zwischen Desplaines- u. Halsted-Str.

☞ Gute Redner werden den neuesten Schurkenstreich der Polizei, indem sie gestern Nachmittag unsere Brüder erschoß, geißeln.

☞ **Arbeiter, bewaffnet Euch und erscheint massenhaft!**

Das Executiv-Comite.

Flyers calling upon workers to arm themselves

There had already been more than a thousand copies of this leaflet distributed before midnight on May 3, and Spies was horrified when he saw the call to arms. He proposed changes to the wording, after which an estimated 20,000 revised flyers were distributed calling for a rally to support workers at 7:30 p.m. the following night, May 4, at Haymarket Square.

Attention Workingmen!

GREAT
MASS-MEETING

TO-NIGHT, at 7.30 o'clock,
AT THE
HAYMARKET, Randolph St., Bet. Desplaines and Halsted.

Good Speakers will be present to denounce the latest atrocious act of the police, the shooting of our fellow-workmen yesterday afternoon.

THE EXECUTIVE COMMITTEE.

Achtung Arbeiter!

Große
Massen-Versammlung

Heute Abend, halb 8 Uhr, auf dem
Heumarkt, Randolph-Straße, zwischen Desplaines- u. Halsted-Str.

☞ Gute Redner werden den neuesten Schurkenstreich der Polizei, indem sie gestern Nachmittag unsere Brüder erschoß, geißeln.

Das Executiv-Comite.

The revised flyer

Haymarket Square in the 1890s

The meeting began the following evening with a rousing speech by Spies, during which he called upon the gathering to remain peaceful: "There seems to prevail the opinion in some quarters that this meeting has been called for the purpose of inaugurating a riot, hence these warlike preparations on the part of so-called 'law and order.' However, let me tell you at the beginning that this meeting has not been called for any such purpose. The object of this meeting is to explain the general situation of the eight-hour movement and to throw light upon various incidents in connection with it."

After Spies was done, it was Parsons' turn, and the subdued manner of his hour long speech put Chicago's mayor, Carter Harrison, Sr., so much at ease that the mayor left in the middle of it, assuming there would be no problems this night. According to the *Chicago Tribune*, however, some members of the crowd remained restless as Parsons spoke: "The most enthusiastic of the crowd were Germans. There was also a large number of Poles and Bohemians, bedsides some American-looking people who came to look on and detectives who had on old clothes. Groups of Germans were discussing the anticipated trouble. Three of these fellow stood right behind the reporter, and he heard their conversation, which they kept up in a not very low tone, although Parsons was talking. 'Our people don't know anything,' one of them said. 'They always shoot in the air when they ought to shoot low. By shooting high they don't hit anybody and often kill one of their own crowd. I have trained in crowds where they knew a thing or two, and our leaders always advised them to aim low.' 'And then, again,' said the second, 'they don't stick together. Haven't Parsons, Spies, and all those fellows told us to stick together? There is where our strength lies.' Several men had their revolvers in their hands under their coats and were prepared for an attack. These drifted around to the northern end of the crowd, where the street was much darker. The windows of the brick building on the northeastern corner of Randolph and Desplaines streets were filled with the heads and faces of men and women."

Mayor Harrison

At about 10:00 p.m., the weather began to get worse as Parsons gave way to the last speaker of the night, a British socialist named Samuel Fielden, and though Fielden only spoke for about 20 minutes, he began to whip up the crowd with a fiery speech: "The Socialists, are not going to declare war; but I tell you war has been declared upon us; and I ask you to get hold of anything that will help to resist the onslaught of the enemy and the usurper. The skirmish-lines have met. People have been shot. Men, women, and children have not been spared by the ruthless minions of private capital. It had no mercy. So ought you. You are called upon to defend yourselves, your lies, your future. What matters it whether you kill yourselves with work to get a little relief or die on the battle-field resisting the enemy? What is the difference? Any animal, however loathsome, will resist when stepped upon. Are men less than snails or worms? I have some resistance in me. I know that you have too. You have been robbed. You will be starved into a worse condition."

Fielden

As Fielden was speaking, police began to gather, and according to a *Chicago Tribune* article the next day, a confrontation quickly started: "At this point those on the outskirts of the crowd whispered 'Police,' and many of them hastened to the corner of Randolph Street. Six or eight companies of police, commanded by Chief Inspector Bonfield, marched rapidly past the corner. Fielden saw them coming and stopped talking.

This proved to be a disaster, and the *Tribune* article described the pandemonium that quickly ensued: "In a few minutes the police from the Desplaines Street station, marching abreast the breadth of Desplaines street, approached. A space of about two feet intervened between each line and they marched silently, so that they were upon the mob almost before the latter knew it. The glittering stars were no sooner seen than a large bomb was thrown into the midst of the police. The explosion shook the buildings in the vicinity, and played terrible havoc among the police. It demoralized them, and the Anarchists and rioters poured in a shower of bullets before the first action of the police was taken. Then the air overhead the fighting mass was a blaze of flashing fire. At the discharge of the bomb the bystanders on the sidewalk fled for their lives, and numbers were trampled upon in the mad haste of the crowd to get away. The groans of those hit could be heard above the rattle of the revolvers. In two minutes the ground was strewn with wounded men. Then the shots straggled, and shortly after all was quiet, and the police were masters of the situation."

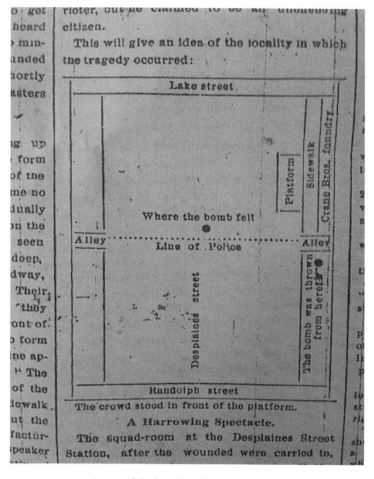

A map of the location of the bomb attack

A contemporary engraving of the bomb going off

Chief Inspector Bonfield gave a fairly similar account: "Finally the speakers urged riot and slaughter; they should have, they said, revenge before morning for yesterday's doings at McCormick's, and revenge on the aristocrats and capitalists for their oppression of the people. They urged all laboring men to arm themselves and not delay the hour of vengeance. I then thought it was time to act and formed the police held in the station in reserve into four companies and, taking them through the side door, marched them in columns up to Randolph street, to where the speaking was going on. Capt. Ward and myself were in front and as we reached the wagon, where a man was speaking, Capt. Ward stepped to the front and said: 'In the name of the State of Illinois I command you peaceable to disperse,' and, turning slightly to each side, he added, 'and I call upon you, and you, to assist.' The crowd gave way and took possession of the sidewalks. Immediately I heard a whizzing in the air above and behind me and then a tremendous explosion. Almost instantly a fusillade of pistol-shots from the sidewalks followed. I ordered the men who were commencing to break to form and then we opened fire." Inspector Bonfield, like the Mayor and the Chief, thinks the police force is able to meet of itself any possible deviltry that the Socialists dare plan or try to execute."

While the *Tribune* and Bonfield suggested the protesters fired at police first, it is still heavily debated whether that's actually the case. Moreover, it is still unknown just who threw the homemade bomb at the advancing police. The article noted the confusion over where the bomb came from: "One of the wounded officers said he saw the bomb come from one of these windows. Officer Marx said he saw the bomb come from the wagon in which the speakers stood."

Either way, the newspaper described the scene as the police began dispersing the fleeing crowd: "When the first shots were fired most of the crowd scattered east and west on Randolph street. The bullets followed the fleeing ones, and many of them dropped on the way before they got out of danger. Quite a number of them ran up towards Halsted Street, and when they had nearly reached it the leader pulled out a huge revolver. He was apparently the same man whom the reporter had heard telling the other two that to stick together was the main thing. 'Stick together,' he cried. 'Come here and let us go and shoot them.' They started towards Desplaines street on a trot, but had only gone a short distance when several shots were fired on the battleground. They turned around and disappeared towards the street from where they had just come. A number of women were also seen in the crowd, and several scampered screaming down Randolph Street. Men were seen falling 500 and 600 feet up Randolph Street, west of Desplaines. Hats were lost, and several, stooping to pick up something they had dropped, were trampled on by the mad mob. In the neighboring stores everything was confusion. Men in their haste to get away from the bullets broke open the doors of the stores and entered, hiding in the first convenient place they could find. The proprietors struck at the intruders with clubs and threatened them with pistols, but they pushed past these and entered."

Not surprisingly, there were a number of journalists there that day, and they offered their own recollection of the scene. One reporter later said, "The police, marching slowly, were in a line with the east and west alley when something like a miniature rocket suddenly rose out of the crowd on the east sidewalk, in a line with the police. It rose about twenty feet in the air, describing a curve, and fell right in the middle of the street and among the marching police. It gave a red glare while in the air. The bomb lay on the ground a few seconds, then a loud explosion occurred, and the crowd took to their heels, scattering in all directions. Immediately after the explosion the police pulled their revolvers and fired on the crowd. An incessant fire was kept up for nearly two minutes, and at least 250 shots were fired. The air was filled with bullets. The crowd ran up the streets and alleys and were fired on by the now thoroughly enraged police. Then a lull followed. Many of the crowd had taken refuge in the halls or entrances of houses and in saloons. As the firing ceased they ventured forth, and a few officers opened fire on them. A dozen more shots were fired and then it cease entirely. The patrol-wagons that had stopped just south of Randolph Street were called up, and the work of looking for the dead and wounded began. The police separated into two columns and scoured the block north to Lake Street and south to Randolph."

Amidst the general confusion, Inspector Bonfield began to worry about his officers inadvertently firing on each other, and he wrote in his report that he "gave the order to cease firing, fearing that some of our men, in the darkness might fire into each other." Another officer admitted to the *Tribune*, "A very large number of the police were wounded by each other's revolvers. ... It was every man for himself, and while some got two or three squares away, the rest emptied their revolvers, mainly into each other." These accounts would bolster the contentions by supporters of the protesters that the police not only fired first but continued to shoot at fleeing civilians.

The mayhem lasted only a few minutes, but it left behind a tragic scene. The same reporter from above recalled, "When the firing had stopped the air was filled with groans and shrieks. 'O God! I'm shot,' 'Please take me home,' 'Take me to the hospital, 'and similar entreaties were heard all over within a radius of a block of the field of battle. Men were seen limping into drug-stores and saloons or crawling on their hands, their legs being disabled. Others tottered along the street like drunken men, holding their hands to their heads and calling for help to take them home. The open doorways and saloons in the immediate vicinity were crowded with men. Some jumped over tables and chairs, barricading themselves behind them; others crouched behind the walls, counters, doorways, and empty barrels. For a few minutes after the shooting nobody ventured out on the street. The dynamite shell did terrible execution among the police. About one-half of those wounded were picked up in the middle of the street where the explosion had occurred. The first to receive attention after the crowd was effectually dispersed were the wounded officers. They were taken to the Desplaines Street Station."

No sooner had the crowds of people who had escaped unharmed reached safety than talk began to spread about the incident. According to the *Tribune*, "After the explosion crowds of excited people assembled on Desplaines, Washington, and Randolph streets, and, with bated breath and compressed lips, talked over the wholesale murder committed by the Anarchists. Hardly a man spoke above a whisper, fearing to identify himself either with the Anarchistic fiends or the law-abiding citizens, as an expression either way meant a broken head and perhaps death. The big bell in the police station tower tolled out a riot alarm, while the telegrapher sent dispatches to other stations calling for aid. Ten minutes later, patrol wagons were dashing toward the scene of the riot from all directions bringing stalwart policemen. The mob shouted wildly as the wagons dashed by, and several missiles were thrown, all of which missed the bluecoats on the wagons. The Anarchists slunk back as a large company of policemen on foot marched down Desplaines street, their faces white with determination and their hands on their revolvers ready to shoot to kill at their commanding officer's order. This company of police marched in front of the station while the dead and dying were being carried in. Several times the mob advanced with wild shouts from the north, but they were kept back as far as Randolph Street."

As the tone of the article clearly indicates, the *Tribune* did not have a lot of sympathy for the protesters, who the paper viewed as having incited the riot, and it very conspicuously identified the rabble-rousers as immigrants: "The Anarchists, led by two wiry-whiskered foreigners, grew bolder and made several attempts to renew the attack but the police held their ground. The wind-bag orators who had harangued the fire-eaters earlier in the evening were not the leaders after business began, but they slunk away and were out of danger. At 11:30, the police made a grand drive at the mob, which was growing larger instead of diminishing. Blank cartridges were fired from hundreds of revolvers in two volleys which set the crowd flying in all directions. The police gave chase as far as the Lyceum Theatre, firing again, and the crowd, covering Madison Street from curb to curb, did not stop running until Halsted Street was passed. This fusillade from the officers practically dispersed the mob, and at 11:45 there were but few people on the streets near the station. After the rioters had been cleared away Desplaines street looked black and deserted, save where the gas-lamps showed blood on the sidewalks and curbstones. The police had the upper hand at midnight. The only citizen wounded whose name could be ascertained was Michael Hahn of No. 157 Eagle Street, who was shot in the back and leg. He was carried into a hallway at No. 182 West Madison Street where he lay groaning. He was able to walk to the patrol wagon, in which he was carried to the County Hospital. He was probably a rioter, but he claimed to be an unoffending citizen."

Many of the injured were police officers, and with the help of their comrades, they made their way to the nearest police station, where they found as chaotic a situation as they had ever experienced on the streets. The *Tribune* explained, "The squad-room at the Desplaines Street Station, after the wounded were carried in, presented a most harrowing spectacle. Half a dozen men from whom the blood literally flowed in streams were stretched upon the floor, others were laid out on tables and benches, and others not so badly wounded were placed in chairs to await with what patience they could the assistance of the surgeons. Mattresses and other bedding were dragged downstairs, and dozens of willing hands did their utmost to assuage the pain of the sufferers. Very soon the doctors were busy with needle, lancet, and probe; priests passed from one wounded man to another, administering brief consolatory words to some and the sacrament of extreme unction to others; officers and volunteer assists went around with stimulants, or helped to bind up wounds or held the patient down while the surgeon was at work, or carried some of the wounded to the other apartments, or in some other way did what could be done to help in easing pain or saving life. Pools of blood formed on the floor, and was trampled about until almost every foot of space was red and slippery. The groans of the dying men arose above the heavy shuffling of feet, and to add to the agony the cries of women—relatives of officers supposed to have been wounded—could be heard from an outer room, beyond which the women were not permitted to enter. Men who had only got a foot or an arm wounded, even though the blood poured from it in streams, sat still, claiming no help in the face of the greater agony. "O, Christ! Let me die!" "O, merciful God!" and similar expressions were continually rung forth as the surgeon's knife or saw was at work or when attempts were made to move those more badly wounded. The priests in attendance were Fathers Kearns, Moloney, Kinsella, Hickey, and Walsh, all from St. Patrick's and Father Byrne from St. Jariath's. The sacrament of extreme unction was administered to eight of the wounded before they were moved from the spot where they had been first laid."

Soon a makeshift hospital was created, consisting of "thirty beds on the upper floor were not sufficient for even the accommodation of the more severely wounded, and several beds had to be made up on the floor. The scene here was as painful as that seen previously on the floor below. The doctors were busy dressing wounds until almost 1 a.m. and it was past midnight before the priests were ready to leave."

One witness at the scene vividly detailed how gruesome the scene was: "Basins of blood were seen at nearly every bedside, and great clots and blotches bespattered the floor, the bed-clothing, and the clothing of those at work as well as of the wounded. Every few minutes, it seemed, a new sufferer was helped into the room, leaning on the shoulders of this brother officers, these later-comers being those who had been slightly wounded, comparatively speaking, and who had rested wherever they could until their brothers were attended to. Two officers were observed bandaging up their own wounds—Peter McCormick and Michael Gordon, the former wounded in the arm and the latter writhing with a fractured foot—but never a moan came from either, each doing what he could for himself until somebody volunteered to help. It seems invidious to select names in this manner where so much heroism was displayed—in fact, to obtain the names of the more heroic was impossible in the excitement and where each hero was perhaps in the agonies of death."

The civilians who had been injured were kept downstairs, surrounding a macabre spectacle. The *Tribune* noted, "In the centre of the room lay the dead body of a Bohemian. A shot had entered his body in the small of the back and had gone clear through him, protruding under the skin. Scattered about just as they were brought in were a dozen men more or less seriously wounded, and waiting for medical attendance. One poor fellow with a flesh-wound in the leg kept up a continuous moaning and screaming, but the remainder were as quiet as the death which was settling down upon not a few of the number."

While many healthy officers were tending the wounded, others were busy trying to restore order in the area. Needless to say, tensions ran high. The *Tribune* concluded, "The cruel heartlessness of the men who exulted over the fact that more than a score of policemen had fallen victims to the deadly Nihilist bomb surpasses belief, and yet it is a fact that, crowded along the sidewalks on both sides of Desplaines street from Madison street to the station, there were hundreds of Communistic sympathizers who exulted in the fiendish work which had been perpetrated but a few moments before. 'served the damned coppers right,' exclaimed a brutal looking hoodlum in front of the Lyceum Theatre, and the next moment he was running for dear life in front of a company of police which came charging down Desplaines street toward Madison brandishing their batons and firing their revolvers in the air. It would have gone hard with any man who should have dared give utterance to such a sentiment as this in the presence of an officer; he would have been killed without a word. As the police by companies swept the streets adjacent to the Desplaines station the mob gave way sullenly and with the worst grace possible, but there was no help for it. …police took it for granted that no man, unless he had had work on hand, would be hanging around the vicinity. For squares from the Desplaines Station companies and squads of offices cleared the streets and mercilessly clubbed all who demurred at the order to go."

An engraving of Officer Mathias J. Degan, who was killed by the bomb

Chapter 3: Indicted for the Murder

"A number of people were arrested and after a time August Spies, Albert R. Parsons, Louis Lingg, Michael Schwab, Samuel Fielden, George Engle, Adolph Fischer and Oscar Neebe were indicted for the murder of Mathias Degan. The prosecution could not discover who had thrown the bomb and could not bring the really guilty man to justice, and, as some of the men indicted were not at the Haymarket meeting and had nothing to do with it, the prosecution was forced to proceed on the theory that the men indicted were guilty of murder because it was claimed they had at various times in the past uttered and printed incendiary and seditious language, practically advising the killing of policemen, of Pinkerton men and others acting in that capacity, and that they were therefore responsible for the murder of Mathias Degan." - Governor John Altgeld

Stirred by incendiary reports carried in the *Chicago Tribune*, the people of Chicago were soon crying out for vengeance against the anarchists and socialists, and authorities quickly arrested Spies and Michael Schwab in the course of searching the offices of their German newspaper, the *Arbeiter-Zeitung*. On May 5, police arrested Oscar Neebe, another member of the newspaper's staff, and they picked up Fielden on the 6th. Parsons only escaped arrest by leaving town quickly.

The edition of the *Arbeiter-Zeitung* the day of the Haymarket Affair

Given that the police still couldn't identify who actually threw the bomb, the pattern of arrests very obviously pointed to the fact that xenophobia was the biggest factor in determining who was arrested. This came within the context of a national fear that immigrants posed a threat with socialist doctrines. In fact, this concern led to the participation of prosecutors from other states. According to the *Chicago Tribune* on May 11, "State's Attorney Grinnell was visited at his office yesterday by State's Attorney Williams of Milwaukee and the two public prosecutors talked over their duties in prosecuting the rioters who took part in the recent outbreaks against law and order in the counties they represent. Mr. Grinnell expressed an unflinching determination to prosecute to the utmost extent of the law the leaders who precipitated the battles on Desplaines and Eighteenth streets and Blue Island Avenue. He said the evidence against these men was strong and satisfactory, but beyond saying that much he did not at present feel justified to speak, for he was not trying their cases in the newspapers."

Regardless of whether the prosecutors intended to try the case in the papers, that would be largely what happened. This is no surprise, especially when readers were being given information that various members of the police force were feeding reporters. The *Tribune* told them, "The officials also had positive evidence as to who threw the bomb, but the reporter's informant refused to state whether or not the guilty person was one of the Anarchists under arrest. Another policeman said it was known that the bomb was thrown by Parsons. ... The examination and cross-examination of the prisoners Fischer, Hirschberg, and Stange, as well as the thousand and one persons who were supposed to know something of their connection with the bomb-throwing, were finished yesterday afternoon. Lieuts. Shea and Kipley agree that their investigation has so far produced excellent results, and that it only remains to work out a few corroborative details to make the case against all the important prisoners a plain one. The idea appears to be that the Spies brothers, Fielden, Schwab, and Parsons, should he be arrested, can readily be convicted of being accessories before the fact. An interesting and vital statement from a party who was present at the time of the explosion, but whose name has been withheld, indicates that Fischer, Stange, and Hirschberg were the secondary actors, who undertook to do the work after it was planned and urged by the leaders. Of these three Fischer and Hirschberg were the most directly connected with the Arbeiter-Zeitung faction, and the former, the police claim, can clearly be proved to have known all about the bomb throwing, and either threw it or stood within reaching distance of the man who did."

As the paper quickly reported, other arrests followed: "Anton Hirschberg, an Anarchistic printer, said to have been connected with the Arbeiter-Zeitung, who was captured in his home at No. 60 Mohawk street last Thursday night by Detective Bonfield, appeared before Justice Meech yesterday morning.... Bonfield said that the police connected the prisoner with the printing of the circulars which called the assembly at the Haymarket last Tuesday night."

One circumstance that would come to have a major impact on the case was the fact that there was a new judge in charge. The *Tribune* noted, "Justice C.J. White, recently of the Desplaines street court, occupied yesterday for the first time the bench of the West Twelfth Street Police Court. ... The most important cases before him were those of three Anarchists named Vaclav and Hynek Dejmek and Frank Nowak. The brothers Dejmek were arrested Saturday last at their home, No. 614 Centre Avenue, and in their rooms were found quantities of materials for the manufacture of dynamite and nitro-glycerine, revolvers, bullets, other warlike materials, and a dynamite tube loaded and capped ready to be used for destructive purposes. Both of the Dejmeks have been in this country nearly seven years, Vaclav having been specially engaged in the circulation of local and foreign Anarchistic publications. They were booked on three charges each – for unlawful conspiracy, for assault with intent to commit murder, and for riot. On the first charge they were held in $1,000, on the second in $3,000, and on the third in $500 each, until the 14th inst. Nowak was held for conspiracy in $1,000 to the same date."

Subsequent police searches also turned up more than enough physical evidence to prove that someone had indeed been making bombs. According to the paper, "About dark last evening some children who were playing under a sidewalk on Clyde Street, near Clybourn Avenue, found two bombs. The attention of a man was called to the fact, and he took the bombs to the Larrabee Station. Officers were sent to the place to hunt for more, but none was found. These bombs are made of a composition resembling lead, and are doubtless of the same kind as that thrown by an Anarchist at Tuesday night's meeting, as pieces of the same kind of material were embedded in the flesh of some of the wounded policemen. The bombs are about three inches in diameter, a quarter of an inch thick, and weigh over a pound. A nut screwed onto a piece of iron fastened to the lower half, and piercing the upper half., keeps the two halves together, the edges fitting closely. A small hole in the side admits the fuse. The inside would hold three or four ounces of explosive material. When taken to the station the bombs were carefully handled, as it was supposed they might be loaded. But the unscrewing of the nuts disclosed that there was nothing in the interior, the surface of which was clean and shiny. Neither bomb had evidently ever been made ready to do its deadly work. Now that it is known that the Anarchists are "planting" the evidence of their crime a vigorous search will be made in all suspected localities, and it is expected that not only bombs and dynamite but guns and revolvers will be found concealed under sidewalks and in other out-of-the-way places."

On May 14, the police arrested Louis Lingg for making explosives, and they also suspected that he had been the one to throw the bomb during the riot, though they apparently did not have enough evidence to make an outright identification.

One of the bombs found in Lingg's apartment

On May 27, a grand jury indicted 12 men for their involvement in the Haymarket Affair. In addition to those already mentioned as having been arrested, they indicted George Engel, Adolf Fischer, Oscar Neebe, Rudolph Schnaubelt, and William Seliger. In their indictment, the jury stated, "We find that the attack on the police of May 4 was the result of a deliberate conspiracy, the full details of which are now in the possession of the officers of the law." Schnaubelt and Seliger escaped prosecution, the former by leaving town and the latter by cooperating with police.

Rudolph Schnaubelt

Chapter 4: Come Into Court

"'Parsons has come into court!' was the announcement that set every one about the Criminal Court Building and police headquarters agape yesterday afternoon. A few moments before 2 o'clock Gerhard Lizius, a former reporter for the Arbeiter-Zeitung, and known to everybody from his arrest in connection with the Socialist agitation, stepped up to hansom cab No. 182 at the corner of Randolph and Clark streets and told the driver to take him to the corner of Morgan and Randolph streets. Arrived there, he told the cabby to draw up in front of the third house south of Randolph, on Morgan, and to head his horse toward the former street. This done, he carefully pulled down the curtains of the cab and then stepped into the house. After a lapse of ten minutes Mrs. Parsons came out, inquired if the cab would carry three, and took a seat in it. Next followed the Anarchist editor himself, who walked down the steps and across the sidewalk holding a handkerchief to his face in order to conceal his features. The reporter then seated himself between them, and the driver was ordered to go to the Criminal Court Building. Mr. Black, the attorney for the defense, was stalking up and down the sidewalk in the sun in front of the Michigan street entrance when the cab pulled up. Parsons jumped out after Lizius, and the attorney and the much-sought editor walked into the building together." - *Chicago Tribune*, June 22, 1886

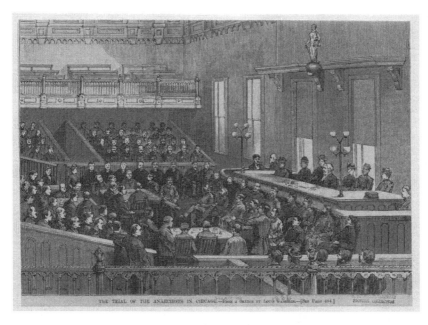

An engraving depicting the trial

The trial process moved much faster in the 19th century than it does in the 21st; on June 21, 1886, less than two months after their alleged crimes were committed, the eight men still in custody in Chicago went on trial. Defending them was Civil War veteran William Black. They were tried together in front of Judge Joseph Gary.

Julius Grinnell, the prosecutor, insisted that Spies was at the heart of the conspiracy to bomb the police. Turning his attention back to the protests on May 3, Grinnell claimed that a plot had been hatched there to incite a rebellion among workers across the city, even as he was forced to admit that the actual bomber had never been identified.

As part of his agreement with the police in order to avoid prosecution, Waller testified against the defendants, and he told the court, "It was said that we ourselves should not participate at the meeting of the Haymarket; we should meet at the respective places; only a committee should be present at the Haymarket, and if they should report that something had happened then we should come down upon them- attack them. ... We have seen how the police oppressed the workingmen, how the capitalists oppress the workingmen, and that six men were killed at McCormick's and that we commence to take the rights in our own hands. ... [A committee was chosen to] observe the movement not only on the Haymarket Square, but in the different parts of the city, and if a conflict should happen then they should report to us."

Later he added that Engel "submitted a plan ... according to which... as soon as it came to a conflict between the police and the Northwestern Groups, that bombs should be thrown into the Police stations and the rifle men of the Lehr and Wehr Verein should post themselves in line in a certain distance and whoever would come out should be shot down."

Ultimately, the most dramatic evidence was offered by H. L. Gilmer, who identified Spies as the man who lit and threw the bomb: "Somebody in front of me out on the edge of the sidewalk there said, 'Here comes the police.' There was a sort of natural rush looking to see the police come up. There was a man came from the wagon down to the parties that were standing on the south side of the alley. He lit a match and he touched it off, something or another it was not quite as big as that, I think, (indicating). The fuse commenced to fizzle, and he gave it a couple of steps forward and tossed it over into the street. ... The man that lit the match on this side of him, and two or three of them stood together, and he turned around with it in his hand, took two or three steps that way, and tossed it that way over into the street. ... Immediately after the explosion, the firing commenced from somewheres around the wagon, in the range of the sound, and was returned by the police. My attention was entirely taken up by the firing and I did not pay attention to anything else afterwards."

During his cross-examination, Black was able to call some aspects of Gilmer's testimony into question, but the damage was still done.

Then, in a strange twist, the mayor of Chicago, Carter Harrison, Sr., testified on behalf of the defense, insisting that the meeting began peacefully enough and that there was no sign of planned trouble. He testified that shortly before the bomb went off, "I went back to the station and stated to Bonfield that I thought the speeches were about to be over; that nothing had occurred yet, or looked likely to occur to require interference, and I thought he had better issue orders to his reserves at that other stations to go home. He replied to me that he had learned the same and reached that conclusion from persons coming and going---he had men out all the time---and had already issued the order; that he thought it would be best to retain the men that were in the station until the meeting broke up.... The order was that the reserves held at the other stations might be sent home, because I learned that all was quiet down in the second district in which McCormick's was; and that I thought there was no design for anything that night. Bonfield replied that he had reached the same conclusion from reports brought in to him, and he had already ordered the reserves elsewhere sent home, or, at least, given them a rest, let them go in their regular order, but that if something might occur yet before this meeting was over or after it, that he would hold the men that were in the station until everything was over. I acquiesced in his suggestion. I didn't give an order. I merely consented to his view. ... I was determined that there should be no re-occurrence of the violence at McCormick's hall; that if there was an overt act, it would be caught in its incipiency and not wait until it took absolute form."

During the trial, Fielden, Spies, and several of the other defendants spoke up for themselves, with Fielden even sharing a portion of the speech he gave that night with the jury. Meanwhile, Spies discussed what happened the night of May 3 after the deadly events of that day: "About eleven o'clock a circular was handed to me to be inserted in the Arbeiter Zeitung, and I looked it over and saw that it was the same meeting where I had been invited to speak. It was this circular [containing the line 'Workingmen arm yourselves and appear in full force'] ... I said to the man 'Is this is the meeting which I have been invited to address, I shall certainly not speak there.' He asked me why, and I told him that that line that it was on account of that line. He said that the circulars had not been distributed, and I told him if that was the case and he would alter the circular, take out that line, then it would be all right; and Mr. Fischer was called down I believe at that time, and he sent a man back to the printing office and as much as I know had the line changed. So far as I know I struck out the line before I handed it to the compositors to put in the Arbeiter Zeitung. ...as far as my knowledge goes, there had none of those circulars been distributed at all."

He also testified that when the police ordered the crowd to disperse, "My brother, and one Lechner, and several others that I didn't know stood at the side of the wagon; and they reached out their hands and helped me off the wagon; I felt very indignant over the coming of the police, and my intention was to ask them what right they had to break up that meeting, but it was certainly very foolish thing for me to do that, and I left the wagon. I jumped down from the wagon. When I reached the sidewalk I heard a terrible detonation, and I thought that the authorities of the city had brought a cannon there to scare away the people from the street. I didn't think they would shoot upon the people, nor did I think in the least at that time of a bomb. That is singular, but I never thought of a bomb having been exploded."

Sigmund Ziesler offered up a popular sentiment shared by many of the defendants and their supporters, complaining that the police "were not heroes, but knaves, led on by the most cowardly knave who ever held public position." Defense attorney William Foster agreed, telling the jury that Parsons could not have known there would be trouble since he brought his wife and children with him to the gathering. Black summed up the final argument by pointing out that six of the eight men on trial were not even at Haymarket that day, and that the two men who were present, Spies and Fielden, were in plain sight on the wagon when the bomb was thrown.

For its part, the prosecution told jurors that the violence, if it went unpunished, would spread across the nation: "The very question itself is whether organized government shall perish from the earth." Grinnell told the jury, "You stand between the living and the dead. You stand between law and violated law. Do your duty courageously, even if the duty is an unpleasant and severe one."

He then rested, and the jury was left to its deliberations on the afternoon of August 19. They reached their verdict before the sun went down, and the next morning, at 10:00, the judge read out: "We, the jury, find the defendants, August Spies, Michael Schwab, Samuel Fielden, Albert R. Parsons, Adolph Fischer, George Engel and Louis Lingg, guilty of murder in manner and form as charged in the indictment and fix the penalty at death. We, the jury, find the defendant Oscar W. Neebe, guilty of murder in manner and form as charged in the indictment and fix the penalty at imprisonment in the penitentiary for fifteen years."

A poster of the seven anarchists sentenced to death

The ink was barely dry on the verdict when the defense filed its first motion, this one for a new trial. It gave two reasons for the request: first, that the jury itself was prejudiced against the accused, and, second, that in no way had the prosecution proved that any of the men had actually made or set off the bomb.

Not surprisingly, Gary denied the motion and proceeded with the sentencing phase of the trial. Before he gave them their sentences, each man was allowed to speak out on his own behalf. Spies was probably the most eloquent, saying in part, "Now, these are my ideas. They constitute a part of myself. I cannot divest myself of them, nor would I, if I could. And if you think that you can crush out these ideas that are gaining ground more and more every day, if you think you can crush them out by sending us to the gallows — if you would once more have people to suffer the penalty of death because they have dared to tell the truth — and I defy you to show us where we have told a lie — I say, if death is the penalty for proclaiming the truth, then I will proudly and defiantly pay the costly price! Call your hangman. Truth crucified in Socrates, in Christ, in Giordano Bruno, in Huss, Galileo, still lives — they and others whose number is legion have preceded us on this path. We are ready to follow!"

Schwab insisted that anarchy was actually a good idea, one that would lead to a more, not less, peaceful world, but Lingg was angry and likely hurt the cause of all those convicted when he cried out, "I repeat that I am the enemy of the 'order' of to-day, and I repeat that, with all my powers, so long as breath remains in me, I shall combat it. I declare again, frankly and openly, that I am in favor of using force. I have told Captain Schaack, and I stand by it, 'if you cannonade us we shall dynamite you.' You laugh! Perhaps you think, 'you'll throw no more bombs;' but let me assure you that I die happy on the gallows so confident am I that the hundreds and thousands to whom I have spoken will remember my words; and when you shall have hanged us, then, mark my words, they will do the bomb-throwing! In this hope do I say to you: 'I despise you. I despise your order; your laws, your force-propped authority.' Hang me for it!"

Neebe, the only one of the group not facing execution, was even more virulent: "I organized trades unions. I was for reduction of the hours of labor, and the education of laboring men, and the re-establishment of the Arbeiter-Zeitung — the workingmen's newspaper. There is no evidence to show that I was connected with the bomb throwing, or that I was near it, or anything of that kind. So I am only sorry, your honor — that is, if you can stop it or help it — I will ask you to do it — that is, to hang me, too; for I think it is more honorable to die suddenly than to be killed by inches. I have a family and children; and if they know their father is dead, they will bury him. They can go to the grave, and kneel down by the side of it; but they can't go to the penitentiary and see their father, who was convicted for a crime that he hasn't had anything to do with. That is all I have got to say. Your honor, I am sorry I am not to be hung with the rest of the men."

In the end, the men's words had no positive impact on the judge, who sentenced them to be "hanged by the neck until dead." However, their attorneys were far from finished, and they quickly filed an appeal with the Illinois Supreme Court, alleging that they had not had a fair trial.

In its ruling, the court chose instead to focus on different questions, saying in its ruling, "The questions which thus present themselves at the threshold of the case, are these: Did the defendants have a common purpose or design to advise, encourage aid or abet the murder of the police? Did they combine together and with others with a view to carrying that purpose or design into effect? Did they or either or any of them do such acts or make such declarations in furtherance of the common purpose or design, as did actually have the effect of encouraging, aiding, or abetting the crime in question?"

In his self-described "inordinately long" opinion, Illinois Supreme Court Justice Benjamin Magruder reviewed focused most of his attention on the evidence rather than procedure and ultimately upheld the conviction on September 14, 1887. He wrote in part:

> "In their lengthy argument counsel for the defense make some other points of minor importance, which are not here noticed. As to these it is sufficient to say that we have considered them and do not regard them as well taken.
>
> "The judgment of the Criminal Court of Cook County is affirmed.
>
> "Be it remembered that afterwards, to-wit: on the 20th day of September, A. D. 1887, the same being one of the regular days of said term of court, certain proceedings were had and orders made by said court and entered of record, among which is found the following, viz:
>
> "August Spies, et al. 59 A.D. vs. The People of the State of Illinois. Error to Criminal Court Cook Co.
>
> "And now on this day come the said plaintiffs in error by William P. Black, their attorney, and move the Court for leave to withdraw the record of the proceedings of the Criminal Court of Cook County filed herein, for the period of thirty days for the purpose of submitting the same to associate counsel, and if so advised to submit the same to the Supreme Court of the United States, upon application for Writ of Error.
>
> "Which said motion is by the Court taken under advisement.
>
> "And now the Court having duly considered said motion and being fully advised of and concerning the premises, overrule the said motion. Therefore it is considered by the Court that the motion for leave to withdraw the record herein filed be and the same is overruled and denied."

The defense then appealed to the Supreme Court, which refused to hear the case because no federal questions were involved.

Chapter 5: They Are Putting On the Caps

"When the intelligence came outside that the men were on the scaffold, the officers who were inside the lines of police went to the northwestern corner of Illinois street and waited. There were in the troup Chief Ebersold, Capt. Schanck, Licui. Kipler, Bold and Blattner and three patrolmen. On the roof of the criminal court building, where they could look through one of the big jail windows, were posted nine policemen and deputy sheriffs. From their position they could see the scaffold and the condemned men upon it. As the given moment approached the men on the roof kept the officers informed of the proceedings inside. As twelve o'clock drew near, a policeman who was straining his eyes to see the interior of the jail raised his hand and without turning his head aside said in a thrilling undertone: 'They are putting on the caps.' For an instant the cluster of officers waited below with bated breath and heads half inclined to one side waiting to hear the noise of the drop. ... A load thump came from the interior of the jail. It was the sound made by the falling trap. Everyone in the group heard it distinctly and everybody knew what it meant. The expectation of the waiters broke up quickly. The policemen, on the root threw down their guns and clapped their hands, and then ceased suddenly, as though ashamed of the act. Captain Schanck flung one arm in the air and smiled feebly. His face was flushed. Chief Ebersold shifted his position, said nothing and then walked quietly away."

Once the defendants ran out of options, the friends of those convicted rallied together to gather 100,000 signatures pleading for their lives. Among those who signed were such luminaries as William Dean Howells, Oscar Wilde, and George Bernard Shaw. The leaders of the Chicago Bar Association also pleaded for clemency, as did other political leaders in Chicago and across Illinois. Overwhelmed by public pressure which included thousands of telegrams from people pleading for and against the men, Illinois Governor Richard Oglesby ultimately decided to grant the requests of Fielden and Schwab to have their sentences reduced to life in prison. The other men had never filed any formal request with Oglesby, so he let their sentences stand.

Oglesby

Friday morning, November 11, 1887, was cold in Chicago but that did not stop a crowd from gathering to see the five men hanged. They were soon surprised to learn that Lingg would not be among them, having chosen to take his own life the previous day with a stick of dynamite that he held in his mouth and lit like a cigar. Though he would linger for several hours with half his face blown off in the explosion, he eventually died and thus escaped the hangman.

Outside of Chicago, the story of the anarchist' last moments spread across the nation: "It lacked just seven minutes and a half of the hour of high noon, when the single white shrouded figure, above which was a face of yellowish pallor—the face of August Spies— passed the first post of the gallows. The command to the crowd fronting the gallows that all must stop smoking was given at 11:35. A dozen or two who were using the weed quenched the fire, some rather reluctantly and the ashes were slowly strewn on the pavements. Whether this command was given out of humanity to the doomed men or as a precaution against the appalling possibility of any treacherous 'bomb lighting in the corridors when the fatal moment came no person seemed aware, but more than one said a prayer down in their inmost hearts. It was now 11:45 and the suspense of the crowd near the gallows was like a slow torture. There was no relief and newspaper men gazed at the gallows and noticed the four ropes swaying slightly to and fro. The gaping crowd, ten feet below, half rose involuntarily from their chairs at the first glimpse of the apparition advancing across the scaffold."

The men walked to gallows under their own power, each attempting to leave some sort of lasting impression with the crowd. The report continued, "Spies looked calm and glanced at the reporters with traces of his old time cynical smile. He walked firmly over the drop, guided by the grasp 'of the deputy, to the furthest end of the gallows. Following close came Fischer, close enough to touch Spies' shroud had his hands not been pinioned under the white muslin. Fischer's countenance had a peculiar glisten, totally unlike the shyness of Engel's heavy featured, and in strong contrast with the dead look of calm in the pinched lineaments of Parsons. The once jaunty, vivacious Texan came last, a withered old man. He had aged twenty years since the day and hour, scarce twelve months before, when he tripped lightly into the court before Judge Gary and flippantly declared that he was ready to be tried at once for his life. The moment his feet touched the scaffold, Parsons seemed to completely lose his identity and to feel that his spirit was no longer part of his body. He had wrought himself to an ecstasy of solemn self-glorification. Only he, the one American, seemed to realize to the full that he must die in a manner to impress, if possible on all future generations the thought that he was a martyr. No tragedian that has paced a stage in America made a more marvelous presentation of a self-chosen part, perfect in every detail. The upward turn of his eyes, his distant faraway look, and...all the attitude of apparent complete resignation that every fold of the awkward shroud only served to make more distinct was far the most striking feature of the entire gallows' picture. The squat form of Engel, alongside...made a hideous contrast of Parson's assumption of the role of a martyr. Fischer was head and shoulders taller than the other three, making his only occasional looks of too-evident bravado more noticeable than might otherwise be, at a...disadvantage compared with the steady coolness of Spies. The latter's quiet, thorough nerve far surpassed as a wonder the demeanor of any of his comrades."

Whatever impression each man wanted to give the audience, he had little time, because those in charge were anxious to get on with the work of the day. "Four...deputies standing to the rear of the four condemned men began without delay to adjust the ropes, Spies' noose being the first one placed. He did not appear to regard it of any more consequence than a new...collar. The knot was slipped down the cord, dose against his neck. Spies did not show a tremor but when the...process was being curried on with Fischer, he turned and quietly whispered to a jailer some suggestions concerning the rope. Fiticher's occasional bravado was quite noticeably lessened when he felt the hempen strand, and...bit his under lip hard when his turn came. Just then Dr. Murphy, a young physician standing back of Engel, whisperingly cracked a joke in Engel's ear. Incredible as it may seem the low-browed anarchist laughed outright with the rope around his neck, and while another was being fastened on Parsons' by his side, but the grotesque laugh stopped in a single instant and Parsons, meekly as a saint, cast big eyes upward at the dangling line above him. Before the four anarchists had an inkling of what was to be done the white caps were deftly slipped upon their heads and drawn quickly down to the neck, shutting off the view of each as completely and with less warning than does the camera cloth of the photographer."

The men being hanged that day were leaders of a movement, not common criminals, and they were anxious to use every last minute of their lives to advance the cause for which they were dying. The article observed, "August Spies was the first of the four doomed men to make most of his wits while he could. In a tone of intense bitterness of spirit, he, the man who wrote the infamous revenge circular, hissed out between his tightly clenched teeth: 'There will come a time when our silence will be more powerful than the voices they are strangling to death.' The last syllables of Spies' concluding words, hoarse with suppressed passion, had not reached an end when Engel raising his voice wildly cried: 'Hurrah for anarchy!' Fischer caught the fire of the utterance and still more loudly exclaimed: 'Hurrah for anarchy!' adding: 'This is the happiest moment of my life.' Then there was a silence like the grave broken abruptly by the slow measured intonation of Parsons like a white robed priest before the altar of sacrifice, not as a dying request, but rather like a command of warning be sounded forth: 'May I be allowed to speak.' Then with a slow enunciation came: 'Will you let me speak. Sheriff Matson?' Then there was another agonizing pause. Muffled through the shroud broke out the unnatural hollow accents: 'Let the voice of the people be heard.'"

Whatever else Parsons was going to say was never heard: "A crash as of a falling house thundered through the corridors. The slender ropes were taut. In full view of two hundred men in front were four white writhing shrouds. The ropes could be seen slowly tightening about the necks that, between the cap and the shroud could be noticed blackening and purpling." As fate would have it, the men would not be granted a swift death: "Nine mortal minutes passed. Then it was known to a certainty that not a neck had been broken. Four Haymarket murderers had been literally throttled and strangled by law."

An engraving of the Execution

Following the deaths of their comrades, Neebe, Schwab and Fielden began serving their sentences, but in 1893, Governor John P. Altgeld, who had replaced Oglesby, chose to pardon them: "Upon the whole, therefore, considering the facts brought to light since the trial, as well as the record of the trial and the answers of the jurors as given therein, it is clearly shown that while the counsel for defendants agreed to it, Ryce was appointed special bailiff at the suggestion of the state's attorney, and that he did summon a prejudiced jury which he believed would hang the defendants, and further, that the fact that Ryce was summoning only that kind of men was brought to the attention of the court before the panel was full, and it was asked to stop it, but refused to pay any attention to the matter, but permitted Ryce to go on and then forced the defendants to go to trial before this jury. While no collusion is proven between the judge and state's attorney, it is clearly shown that after the verdict and while a motion for a new trial was pending, a charge was filed in court that Ryce had packed the jury, and that the attorney for the state got Mr. Favor to refuse to make an affidavit bearing on this point, which the defendants could use, and then the court refused to take any notice of it unless the affidavit was obtained, although it was informed that Mr. Favor would not make an affidavit, but stood ready to come into court and make a full statement if the court desired him to do so."

He also pointed out, "No matter what the defendants were charged with, they were entitled to a fair trial, and no greater danger could possibly threaten our institutions than to have the courts of justice run wild or give way to popular clamor, and when the trial judge in this case ruled that a relative of one of the men who was killed was a competent juror, and this after the man had candidly stated that he was deeply prejudiced and that his relationship caused him to feel more strongly than he otherwise might, and when in scores of instances he ruled that men who candidly declared that they believed the defendants to be guilty; that this was a deep conviction and would influence their verdict, and that it would require strong evidence to convince them that the defendants were innocent, when in all these instances the trial judge ruled that these men were competent jurors, simply because they had, under his adroit manipulation, been led to say that they believed they could try the case fairly on the evidence, then the proceedings lost all semblance of a fair trial."

Then there was the matter of the lack of evidence against each man. This led the governor to note, "It is now clear that there is no case made out against Fielden for anything that he did on that night, and, as heretofore shown, in order to hold him and the other defendants for the consequences and effects of having given pernicious and criminal advice to large masses to commit violence, whether orally, in speeches or in print, it must be shown that the person committing the violence had read or heard the advice, for until he had heard or read it he did not receive, and if he never received the advice it cannot be said that he acted on it. ... Now, with all of the eagerness shown by the court to convict Neebe, it must have regarded the evidence against him as very weak, otherwise it would not have made this admission, for if it was a debatable question whether the evidence tended to show guilt, then that evidence must have been far from being conclusive upon the question as to whether he was actually guilty; this being so, the verdict should not have been allowed to stand, because the law requires that a man shall be proven to be guilty beyond a reasonable doubt before he can be convicted of a criminal offense. I have examined all of the evidence against Neebe with care and it utterly fails to prove even the shadow of a case against him. Some of the other defendants were guilty ef using seditious language, but even this cannot be said of Neebe."

Taking all the evidence presented to him in total, Altgeld ultimately concluded, "I am convinced that it is clearly my duty to act in this case for the reasons already given, and I, therefore, grant an absolute pardon to Samuel Fielden, Oscar Neebe and Michael Schwab this 26th day of June, 1893."

Altgeld

The human drama surrounding the defendants of the Haymarket Affair may have come to an end with that, but the impact would last much longer, and it would remain politically charged. Throughout the rest of the decade, the labor movement only grew stronger, and trade unions kept up the call for an 8 hour work day and general strikes each May Day, May 1. As historian Nathan Fine has pointed out, "[T]he fact is that despite police repression, newspaper incitement to hysteria, and organization of the possessing classes, which followed the throwing of the bomb on May 4, the Chicago wage earners only united their forces and stiffened their resistance. The conservative and radical central bodies – there were two each of the trade unions and two also of the Knights of Labor — the socialists and the anarchists, the single taxers and the reformers, the native born...and the foreign born Germans, Bohemians, and Scandinavians, all got together for the first time on the political field in the summer following the Haymarket affair.... [T]he Knights of Labor doubled its membership, reaching 40,000 in the fall of 1886. On Labor Day the number of Chicago workers in parade led the country."

Johannes Gelert's statue of a Chicago policeman was erected in Haymarket Square in 1889

A picture of the Haymarket Martyr's Monument, erected in 1893 at the grave site of the defendants

Eventually, of course, the labor movement would triumph on the issue that led to the Haymarket Affair, and in the 120 years that have since passed, leaders have tried to strike a more balanced tone when commemorating the important events of 1886. When Chicago installed a bronze plaque at the site of the Haymarket Affair in 1992, it read, "A decade of strife between labor and industry culminated here in a confrontation that resulted in the tragic death of both workers and policemen. On May 4, 1886, spectators at a labor rally had gathered around the mouth of Crane's Alley. A contingent of police approaching on Des Plaines Street were met by a bomb thrown from just south of the alley. The resultant trial of eight activists gained worldwide attention for the labor movement, and initiated the tradition of 'May Day' labor rallies in many cities."

Online Resources

Other 19th century history titles by Charles River Editors

Other Chicago history titles by Charles River Editors

Other titles about the World's Fair on Amazon

Bibliography

Fireside, Bryna J. (2002). *The Haymarket Square Riot Trial: A Headline Court Case*. Berkeley Heights, N.J.: Enslow Publishers.

Harris, Frank (1908). *The Bomb*. London: John Long.

Lum, Dyer (1887). *A Concise History of the Great Trial of the Chicago Anarchists in 1886*. Adamant Media Corporation.

Parsons, Lucy (1889). *Life of Albert R. Parsons: with brief history of the labor movement in America*. Chicago: L. E. Parsons.

Smith, Carl (1995). *Urban Disorder and the Shape of Belief: The Great Chicago Fire, the Haymarket Bomb, and the Model Town of Pullman*. Chicago: University of Chicago Press.

Made in the USA
San Bernardino, CA
13 October 2018